The quiet Republican
Cherilyn G. Hearn

The quiet Republican ~ Cherilyn G. Hearn ~ c.2014

dedicated to
all the quiet Republicans
and
Grandpa

1

She Speaks

There are probably millions of books on politics, maybe more. It's my guess, just a guess, that most of these are stating one side or the other and vehemently making their opinions or at least what they perceive to be a certain party's opinion clear and why it is so incredibly right or so incredibly wrong. I'd like to think that is not what this book will say. In case you haven't guessed, I am a Republican. But like choosing a scoop of ice cream, I don't think my flavor is the only flavor, the best flavor or of superior historical importance. It's just mint chip. To each his own.

So why the book? I guess I feel like my journey has been curious, bumpy, but quiet. I think there may be others like me out there or even others out there who don't know who they are politically and maybe this book will help them find their way. Maybe my book will make someone realize they are the exact opposite. Perfect.

For a long time, I did not truly know my political affiliation. I have always thought I was a Republican. I came to this conclusion because of my conservative side and I guess, some youthful assumptions on my part. I am Pro-Life and a Christian. I believe in traditional male, female roles in the home and I come somewhat from a white collar, privileged family.

However, I don't judge. I have gay friends and I couldn't care less if they want to get married. I don't believe in abortion, but I don't scream murder in anyone's faces. I feel sorry for the poor and I will give them money if I have it, but usually, I'm poor too. My idea of poor may be a little off and of course, relative.

I've asked several people lately, what are the big differences between Democratic and Republican? The differences in their answers offered no help in my search for a definition for myself. Some of them immediately started talking about the election, the candidates, the mud-slinging. This was no help. Others took me on a history lesson, going as far back as FDR and JFK. This was no help. I started to wonder if anyone knew or if there was one clear definition.

As I listened to the first of many presidential debates for the 2012 election, it seemed to me that both men just went back and forth, objecting to what their opponent had just said and restating what they had already said, over and over. I sometimes wonder if presidential campaigns are simply months of confusing the voters and ultimately the most popular candidate winning, based on things that have nothing to do with the real issues.

Sadly, I don't see how anyone in Washington D.C., from congressmen and women, to the President and his opponents, has any idea what life is like for the average American like you and me. I think they travel around and shake hands and have conversations, but at the end of the day, they have no clue what my day is like, how their decisions affect my life, my children, my stress level.

How can politicians even stand behind the podium talking about lowering taxes, cutting deficits and changing lives, while they still attend their gluttonous parties and spend ridiculous amounts of money decorating the White House? This just shows me how far they are from me and my life. But I digress. This is supposed to be about me and my struggle to find political identification and affiliation within my own identity.

I have always dubbed myself the quiet Republican, primarily because it seems you always *hear* Republicans and I don't see myself as that type of constituent. Funny to me, Republicans are known to be conservative, classy, stoic; all things I relate to in my own personality. But when I read, see and hear Republicans, none of those words spring to mind. Ironically, since my sad departure from being one of my parents' dependents, I have also never been very well off, but I was raised under their political umbrella and no matter how much the Democratic party crusades to help the poor and work for social reform, I have never quite seen myself as belonging to that society. Am I crazy or just in denial?

A couple of years ago, I worked on a political campaign for a state senator, running for U.S. Congress. Being in a primarily Republican state and district, she ran on the Republican ticket, but was admittedly liberal and it was well known that her political party choosing had more to do with her location and likelihood of being elected, than her true beliefs. I found this to be incredibly confusing and wondered how many other people in political office were in the closet. When the votes don't always match the seat, what does this mean for our country? I served her campaign loyally, because I did believe in most of her views, but the backstory always left me befuddled.

So is that what I am doing? Am I a fraud? Do I wear a Republican hat, however discreet, but deny the benefits I receive from Democratic actions? I say no to fraud and yes to my hat, but that it is irrelevant. If the Democratic Party and its programs disappeared tomorrow, I would fall on the things my parents taught me and I would still feel the same about the issues that I have strong feelings for. That leads me to another point, what about the variety of things I really don't care about? Does that make me a bad American? I don't think so. It does, however, worry me that my party has opinions that I am simply ignorant of, but I still claim their platform as my own. I fear this is true for many Americans. We have no idea what some of our rotten apples may be out there doing to our bunch.

It is my sad opinion that so many Americans do not understand politics, most of the issues or a great deal of things that politicians say and do. That is a huge statement to the success of the past and the state of the future of our country. Neither of which look that promising when you think of it in that context. Politicians are out of touch, so far removed from the people they claim to be protecting, leading and fighting for. They are them and we are us. The haves and the have nots? I own a home and a car. I have a good retirement set up. I am still not in the same reality as *any* politician from *any* party. This is not how it should be. When you think back, this is not how the forefathers started out. Or is that just how the history books tell it?

As the debate finished up, our Democratic president tapped into our heart strings and told some touching stories about people across the country he had met and the stories he has been told. I felt this was a little bit of a ploy and I could almost hear the sappy music chiming in the background. The Republican candidate was all business, restating a lot of his campaign messages and familiarizing the viewers with his record as a Governor of his respective state. There they stood in their expensive suits and red and blue ties, standing behind shiny mahogany podiums before rushing off to their waiting limousines. Who are these people and why are they leading our country? They don't know *me* at all.

So, I'm writing this book in 2014, in preparation for a book tour in 2015. Coincidentally, 2016 will be an election year. So, I vow to be diligent, to research, to know some things about *both* parties. I truly want this book to be an enlightenment. One of our stops on the tour is Washington D.C. This should be fun.

So, you know, really, your political affiliation is who you are, even if you never vote. A hamster can say it isn't a hamster all day, but it just is. So the key is to study both parties and see where you land. No worries...if you don't land in box A or box B, there are more boxes! There are even tests on Google where you answer ten questions and it will tell you what you are. But that's a little too simple for me. I don't just want a bumper sticker. I want to know, to understand, to identify and believe. I'm hoping to help my readers get to the same place in a non-comatose, sometimes comical way. After all, politics is so boring! Right?

What if you don't care about politics or what your political affiliation may or may not be? You've gotten along fine until now right? Maybe. I guess it's like a gene floating around in your body. You have something, good, bad or indifferent, you have it. Maybe you'll never need it, maybe you will. Maybe it will suddenly be relevant in the blink of an eye. Don't you want to know the answer, to know *what you are?*

Most of all, I hate not having a concrete reason for my ideas and beliefs. If someone asks you what your religion is, who you root for in the game, why you're a Vegetarian; if you say "I dunno," I promise, you have just lost some brain points in their book. We really should never call ourselves anything and not have a reason, a story. You know how people always say not to bring up religion or politics? That's why. So many people do not have an answer, do not know why, do not want to admit that their preferences this week have to do with someone's cheating husband or someone else's ugly wife. These are not reasons for taking one side one side or another politically. Or are they? I ask a lot of questions in this book. Most of them, I will not answer. I think sometimes, getting readers to ask questions of themselves is much more meaningful than answering them. I mean, really....who cares what my answer is?

This is America where we are FREEEEEE!!! We hear that all the time don't we? We're not free to cross on the red or not pay taxes or smack our annoying neighbor, but we're free right? So...what if someone just votes for <u>anyone</u> running against Hillary, because they see her as a joke for staying with Bill thinking it means she is weak, has no backbone or no self-respect? (I'm sorry, was that my heart I left Gorilla-Glued to my sleeve?) They may be wrong, they may be right, but they absolutely *can* vote on that basis. That said, why would they need to know the importance of claiming one political affiliation or another if they clearly have other means for deciding their vote? Here's why. After the dust has settled and the ballots are counted, a victor will be announced. Then, for four years or two years or for whatever term our hypothetical candidate holds office, many things will happen that have nothing to do with cheating husbands, hunting Elk, middle names or where someone may or may not have been born. These things that are going to happen, are things we may have been able to predict and consider before we dropped our ballot, if only we had known . . . .

For the purpose of staying on track, when I do reference current events, I will most likely focus on the Presidential office, simply because it affects everyone and I can't possibly touch on every political office in the land. BUT. . . I do watch CNN and when things come up, if I can see a place for them, you can bet I'll include it. This is only 2014, but already there is a lot of talk of what the country will be in for during the 2016 campaigns and election.

> Not So Fun Fact: In a Freshman High School class in Kansas in 2013, of the fourteen students in World History ~ four of them state that they do not know the difference between Republicans and Democrats. Four claim to be Republican. Four claim to be undecided. Zero are Democrat, but this is Kansas. ;)

Now I will go do some digging.

~

Who are you? You cannot simply say that you don't care or you have no political party. I mean, you can, but you'll just be speaking incorrectly. Don't let your actions, your neighborhood, your clothes or your habits go around inaccurately speaking for you. Own it.

Below I'm going to list some hot topics that are usually very black and white as far as what side of the political arena you reside on. In your mind, you know where you are. You may not admit it at a cocktail party or write it down in a class, but right now, reading this book, in your head your voice will scream out a resounding opinion. In later chapters, we will dig deeper and determine if these opinions alone, can define your political party.

I also have some musings about the upcoming 2016 Presidential Race.

How do you feel about...

Abortion?
Firearm rights? (To purchase, own, use, etc.)
Immigration?
Stem cell research?
Right to Life? (Euthanasia, etc.)
WAR? (Military...action, inaction, pay & benefits)
Death Penalty?
Gay Marriage?
Religious Freedom (church & state)
Men & Women (in the home, in the workplace, in the military)

You're already feeling the wagons circle aren't you? You're already mounting your cases…for or against. *What is this lady going to say? Will I be against her? Will we agree?* Regardless if you are an impassioned forensic thinker, you have opinions and they're already starting to rumble…

More later.

~

So, really…it's a little hilarious that I am writing this book. But as I comb the internet for good, solid information, even as I laugh at myself, I am excited to think how much I am going to learn, in my effort to enlighten others. I do NOT know a lot about politics! *Go* ahead, check the cover, yes….I am the author of *The Quiet Republican*. Make no mistake. But anyone can learn. Anyone can research. Anyone can find out who they are. Even you.

`Sidebar:` Forgive me now if I write beneath you or over you. I try to find a happy place in the middle, but readers are relative and that's a melting pot. You WILL find yourself saying, "duh, everyone knows that" AND "hello! Not everyone knows that!" Dust off your hurt feelings and move on. Everyone is different. I want to be read and understood by as many people as possible! I apologize in advance.

Politics are ongoing. I mean I already said we are political in our hearts every day, but I mean the real CNN stuff. The minute one race ends, in some way, preparation for the next race begins. So this is February of 2013 and plans and talk and yes, campaigning for 2016 is well underway! So naturally I use the internet, the biggest bird's nest there is! I look at everything, because even unreliable information teaches us something; about people, about opinions, about the power of the written/spoken word. I will be uber honest about my sources and how credible I find them to be. Of course I am a writer, so every opinion has merit. Even nonsense may be the most finely crafted nonsense out there.

So I found the following rumored candidates for President in 2016. This means they have either flat out said they're running, or political analysts predict it or just some person with a column or a blog thinks they might. I will try and focus on the first two!

(In no particular order.)

Republican Governor Rick Perry of Texas ~ I have heard of this person and he seems to be a realistic possibility to run. He is the longest serving Texas Governor ever, serving currently and since December, 2000, but has already announced retirement after 2014. That's fourteen years power in one state, but it takes more than one state loving you to be President. So let's say he gets Texas. Will *some* people not vote for him because they hate Texas, because they hate the Cowboys, because they don't like his new glasses? Yes, that will absolutely happen.

Democrat Vice President Joe Biden ~ Obviously turning a Vice-Presidency into a spot on the ticket is reasonable and predictable, BUT Obama may be the most hated President of all time. This can work for *and* against his second in command. In his corner, the fact that Obama has had so much attention good and bad. I can't think of one thing I have heard of Joe Biden doing, at all, for the last six years. So I guess no news is good news?? On the other hand, Obama haters will be Biden haters, regardless of his stance on the issues, his education, his records, etc. There are also people that will vote for him because he reminds them of their favorite Grandpa. This is sad, but this *is* politics.

Republican John Ellis "Jeb" Bush ~ Do you know who Jeb Bush is? He's the former Governor of Florida. He's also former President George W. Bush's brother & former President George & Barbara Bush's other son. The *other son, the brother*...these are stigmas he would face during any kind of campaign. He was even quoted on www.politico.com as saying that his "family name would be an issue" in running for President. Like Biden, would he simply have the support of his brother and father's supporters and not be appreciated by their opponents? Would *his* life, *his* history, *his* platform even be considered?

Republican New Jersey Governor, Chris Christie ~ Chris Christie is a leading member of the Republican Party, according to Wikipedia.com. He is pretty much guaranteed to run for President in 2016 according to rumors, the internet, www.thewire.com, etc. He has partnered with the Bush camp on many issues and events in his career. Of late, he is being railroaded for closing a lane on a bridge. Huh? Ok, admittedly, that's all I know about it, but that's all I care to know. It's a lane, on a bridge...who cares! If that's the worst thing he's ever done.... Also in the headlines, in preparations for a better image as a presidential candidate, he has recently had lap band surgery. So, will he be immediately loved by some overweight constituents for that reason alone? Will some skip over his name because it sounds like a girl's first name? Yes.

Republican Mike Huckabee ~ Mike Huckabee is the former Governor of Arkansas. Not a typical politician, Huckabee is also an ordained minister, an author, a radio personality and has his own television show. So let's just toss that into the pot! He has also run for president before, but was beaten in the primaries by John McCain. Is Huckabee truly a Renaissance Man or just a Jack of all trades and master of none? Will he have the Christian vote on blind faith? Will he be blanket judged by the non-religious?

Republican Congressman Paul Ryan ~ In the 2012 election, Ryan served as Vice-Presidential running mate to Republican candidate Mitt Romney. Guilty! That's all I know about the guy. In a sea of Republicans, will he sink or swim?

Democrat & former Secretary of State, Hillary Clinton ~ Hillary Clinton was surely first known globally as the First Lady to her husband for President Bill Clinton. She was both shamed and heralded when he was found to have had some type of affair while in office, with White House intern and previous 'nobody' Monica Lewinsky. Since her husband's time in office, she has been doing her own thing, serving as a New York Senator and then as the U.S. Secretary of State, under President Barack Obama. Before 1968, Hillary was a Republican. The most glaring detail about Clinton is that she is a woman. Perhaps this is why her resume includes her championing issues like foster care and adoption and why we hear about her haircuts and her wardrobe in the news. Clinton ran and narrowly lost to Presidential Nominee Barack Obama in 2008 and she is named by many as a shoe-in for the next President and the first ever female President of the United States. So…will she be elected by women everywhere, simply out of sisterhood? Will Clinton supporters vote for her based on her name alone? Besides the Vice President, she is the only prominent Democrat I have found to be considering running for President in 2016. A quote from www.politico.com described Clinton as "a product of Washington." She will be judged based upon her cheating husband, her awkward daughter and her fluctuating weight and how it affects the fit of her pant suits. There is a fairly new television show called Scandal. Supposedly just a fictitious television show like any other, but with some very close-to-home story lines. In any case, one of the characters is a female vice president, who could be described as looking and sometimes acting a lot like Hillary Rodham Clinton. There are voters who dislike that character, on tv and will therefore be anti-Hillary, even and especially if they have zero political knowledge whatsoever. That's a fact.

Politics are so incredibly personal. You cannot remove yourself from politics.

There was a great bar graph on www.2016election.com, listing possible candidates by last name only, in order of popularity, as in, who had the best chances of victory. I read nothing else but the graphs.

<u>Republican</u>
Christie
Cruz
Paul
Bush & Ryan (tied)
Rubio

<u>Democrat</u>
Clinton
Biden
Warren
Cuomo, Booker & O'Malley (tied)

Interesting.

So, surely there are more. I don't suggest that I have named everyone, just getting the wheels turning. Why so many Republicans? Can I tell you my guess? Two reasons.

(1)　We are sadly coming off of eight rough years in the White House. Regardless of the details, the bad apples have fallen from a

Democratic tree and Republicans are chomping at the bit to get back in the Oval Office. Some of them may even be in cahoots, to simply flood the options with Republicans, to saturate the minds of the voters.

(2) Hillary Clinton is wildly popular and no other Democrat thinks they can beat her, so why bother trying. Running against her may mess up their chances of having her as an ally later on.

Lots of things to think about so far. So many things go into the why and the how of American Politics, from the people to the candidates. The candidates are people and the people can be candidates, but in an election year, a line is drawn.

2

Women's Issues? Let's Get Sentimental

As promised, let's start digging into the issues, the pros and the cons and which parties support what.

Abortion

I see no reason to beat around the bush, let's just get this one out of the way. Republicans are pro-life and Democrats are pro-choice. Period. Yes we can pick it apart and talk about the various scenarios and gray areas, but that is basically the truth of it. Some Republicans base their steadfast position on life and the argument of when it begins, some come from a place of faith and strictly stand behind the Bible on this issue. I don't mean to belittle the many ways in which the issue can branch out, but my purpose is to define the two parties as plainly as I can. There are exceptions to every rule.

We see a lot of politicians tip toe around this issue, finding ways to ride the fence and talk about the what ifs and maybes. This is because they don't want to alienate themselves. They don't want to be totally denied by either side. This is true on a lot of issues, but perhaps none as much as abortion. This type of passion can be found in matters of the heart, when things get personal, when government issues become family issues.

I am pro-life, period. I cannot think of a situation where abortion is acceptable. That said, I would not personally, face to face tell someone else not to have an abortion *unless they asked me* and even then, my words would be polite. I wouldn't call anyone a murderer or hold a sign or block an entrance. That's just not me. It's not my place to judge and they have to live with themselves. If there was a law on the ballot to make abortion illegal across the board, I would support it. If I myself were pregnant and the doctor said I would die if I continued the pregnancy, I would take my chances and pray. I would counsel my daughters to do the same. Putting my life before that of my child, is the definition of motherhood.

I have friends who are pro-choice and this does not interfere with our friendship. I have friends who have had abortions, etc. My mother had an abortion when I was three months old. So, it crosses my mind that I could have been aborted and that my only full sibling was and that relationship was taken from me. I have a medical condition that makes it hard for me to get pregnant. I have given birth to one child and have had miscarriages.

So, all of these things about me surely add to my stance on abortion. Would my feelings be the same if only one of those experiences existed? We'll never know. The point is, everyone has life experiences. Everyone. Even the President. None of us can separate our personal feelings from our political ones. It's impossible.

Gun Control

Again, always start with the cut and dry, black and white, basics. Then we can pick things apart. Republicans believe in the right to bear arms. Democrats believe in more gun regulation. It's no secret that the Republican Party is known as the GOP, which stands for Grand Old Party. So you will start to notice a trend in their ideas and thinking, as originating in the foundation set up by our forefathers over two hundred years ago. The *age* associated with their party and their opinions is sometimes viewed as outdated, non-progressive and not in-sync with a changing and growing America in these modern times. As usual, there are two sides to every story. If you start deciding that old is bad, then is the Constitution bad? The Bill of Rights? The Bible?

I think I have the right to own a weapon and if my name doesn't ring any bells, it should be fairly easy to acquire. There are some types of high powered weapons that I don't think need to be accessible to the public; that should be provided to military and law enforcement only. BUT, there are rotten apples in every bunch and I have no doubt, some of those weapons would eventually end up in the wrong hands. But this isn't about me, necessarily.

If you're struggling with the issues, the only person you need to talk to, is you.

Do you own a gun or want to own a gun? Why or why not?

Have you been the victim of a crime or ever been in fear for your safety? If not, do you think your opinion or desire would change if you did find yourself in one of those situations?

Is there something in your past that makes you anti-guns? I know I said we can never separate our personal feelings from our political points of view, and that is true, but if you *do* think your opinion may be swayed due to a specific experience, just knowing that and identifying that in your mind is important when making decisions and even judgments about political platforms and others opinions. It's impossible to just remove these characteristics from our personalities. But the more we are aware that they exist, the more evolved we are and the more unbiased our decisions become.

Stem Cell Research

What? Believe it or not, in some circles, stem cell research is as hot a topic as abortion. But since it has spent a little less time on the front page, let's start with a mini lesson on the topic.

The controversial side of stem cell research lies in the embryonic cells. There are adult cells, which an adult can consent to using; cord cells, which a parent can consent to after the cord has been removed from a baby; and embryonic cells, which are cells within an embryo before it is considered viable. The controversy exists because these cells can be created by fertilizing eggs in a lab, which starts to touch on the topic of when life begins, cloning, abortion, etc. So you can basically apply the abortion beliefs, with regard to political parties, to the topic of stem cells. Embryonic cells are considered to be human beings by Republicans and just some stuff in a test tube by Democrats.

I know I sound harsh and I know it's more complicated than that. Please read my whole book or none at all before you send me some hate mail.

Surely there are Democrats and Republicans alike who would not put it as bluntly as that, but I reject those type of explanations. You're either for it, or against it. When you tip-toe around it, throw in some what ifs and maybe...you're just riding the fence, remember?

Once in a while, for kicks, we'll examine the potpourri that eventually becomes of every worthwhile topic in the media, in the world, on the minds of the people that make things happen or *not* happen. But not this time.

Young or Ignorant? In a seventh grade biology class, none of the students knew what stem cell research was. After a brief, brief explanation of the embryonic issue, four of them thought embryonic research to be acceptable. The remaining six students were undecided.

Right To Life

The right to life addresses a variety of situations, from the decision to cease medical equipment for a comatose patient, removing food from a patient with no quality of life or actually assisting someone in their own death when their diagnosis is terminal or bleak.

In Chapter Four we'll talk about miracles and how the belief in a higher power effects EVERY issue we're talking about in this book.

Once again, we now have three topics that center around the definition of life. Abortion, stem cell research and the right to life are all issues whose supporters and opponents are divided based on their definition of 'life.' Because this is a repeating scenario, I've decided to make somewhat of a chart below, making the lines between life & death, Republican and Democrat, glaringly clear.

Republicans…	Democrats…
Life is life.	Life is relative and can be measured according to quality.
A beating heart & a fertilized egg are both living things worth protecting	Not every beating heart is connected to a worthwhile brain & body

Life begins at birth |
| Anti-Abortion
Anti-Embryonic Stem Cell Removal
Anti-Euthanasia | Pro-Choice
　　Pro-Research
Pull the plug |

Even as a quiet Republican, I do think it's unfortunate how these three issues have intertwined, somewhat forcing the hand of anyone with a strong opinion on any one of them. Politics does that. You may have a very strong opinion about abortion. Maybe you have a personal experience or something in your life or your surroundings that makes you particularly passionate about that issue. However, maybe you know nothing about stem cells and have never considered your opinions on right to life. No matter. You stance on abortion says something to your definition of life and therefore, your place on the other two issues is assumed based on that.

It's not that I don't see the connection, I may even agree with it. I just don't ever like assumptions being made. So, are there assumptions about your position on any of these topics, out there being made because you've been outspoken on just one of them?

These are ALL issues about life and one's definition of what that means. Recently, a famous comedian killed himself. Naturally it was all over the news, social media, late night television, etc. Of course there was the shock and the grief, but there was also the criticism, the irony of someone who spread laughter and mirth actually drowning in a sea of unhappiness. There was also the predictable "selfish" debate. Suicide is always said to be soooo "selfish!" Really? So, if I am drowning, I should keep flapping my arms and gasping and trying, to make YOU feel better? To just succumb and sink, makes me selfish? Hmmm.

So, some would say, having been so reckless with "life," those who commit suicide are also likely to support abortion, the death penalty and euthanasia. Sound right?

Military & War

There are many things about the government that a lot of people don't understand, including me. It's not an insult, it's just a fact. There's a lot of things about computers and combustions engines and German I don't understand either. It doesn't mean we lack intelligence, it's just life. That said, it's important to be open to those possibilities, that we don't know everything, that there are things that go on that we may not consider, that we maybe cannot even imagine. Once again, this doesn't need to dominate your thinking, but rather just float in the background, keeping you open and receptive.

No one wants their child or their spouse to go somewhere where people will be plotting to hurt them. This is reasonable. The Democrats and our Democratic President are for having the troops in foreign countries, handling foreign problems, under the guise that in the big picture, their peace is best for the well-being of the United States. This is one topic that can fluctuate quite a bit based on the location, the conflicts and what other contributing factors may be going on. EVERYONE remembers it was a Republican administration that started the war, but how long ago was that again?? Some of my Democratic chums insist that Obama is getting the troops out "as fast as he can." HA! He's the president. If he wanted, they would be home for supper.

The easy way to remember is this. Democrats are often described as "bleeding-heart liberals." Not by me necessarily, but I've heard this in a circle or two. So, if you subscribe to that logic, they are about helping other countries, solving other people's problems, fixing everything, etc. Republicans are pro-U.S at all times. Let the rest of the countries do what they please. As long as our borders are secure, let's just keep our troops at home. Over the course of history there have been a few exceptions, but this is a tool to find out which camp you're in.

Some people compare military work to law enforcement and emergency responders. They too have dangerous jobs, but the difference is that they are here, defending, protecting and administering care to Americans. Aren't they?

Here is something to ponder. We will discuss immigration later, but when police officers and firemen are dispatched to any situation, they have no idea if the people they are dealing with are immigrants (legal or illegal), tourists or terrorists. Yet they are supposed to treat everyone with the same set of laws.

Is this fair?

Is this dangerous?

Is sending Americans to the other side of the tracks or the other side of the world the same or totally different? We pay taxes for the protection of law enforcement. Why then are we not treated better than illegal immigrants or tourists? I know the obvious answer. It's asking the question that matters.

So we've pushed some red hot buttons. Do you know who you are yet? There are more issues to cover, but let's take a break and talk about how our personal lives lend to our political affiliation.

3

Conservative Is As Conservative Does

In the same way that we cannot hide our personal views from our politics, we cannot keep politics out of our personal lives. If someone didn't know you, but just knew a handful of things about you, they could make a pretty fair assumption about your politics, even if you can't.

This can be applied to our relationships and our community. We're going to explore some hypotheticals that you may or may not recognize and then, yes, I will tell you all about me.

What is the definition of conservative? Of course we can Google it and find something brilliant on Wikipedia, or go old school and see what Webster says. But truly, conservative means different things to different people and within a certain boundary, they would all be correct. If it walks like a duck and quacks like a duck...

Do you walk and talk and live like a Conservative? Do you think you're conservative, but your actions prove otherwise? Are you living one life, but in your heart, you believe in the opposite? If you're reading this book, these may be issues of self-identity that you are struggling with or are just curious about. So let's try and get some answers.

I cannot promise that my views do not slip through in the pages I am writing. Like politics, it can be difficult to keep my personality out of anything I write, especially non-fiction. That said, I do hope to convey a number of sides and allow my readers to find theirs. When my opinion is completely transparent, that's the time to just know that I am who I am and you are who you are. We will always encounter opposing perspectives in our life. See this as an opportunity to broaden your horizons, rather than put up your dukes. ☺ I am not trying to convince anyone of anything, to be Republicans or Democrats. You see, my point is that you can't convince anyone of a political party, any more than you can convince them what their favorite ice cream is.

Maybe, maybe when people are somewhat young, high school and college, you might be able to educate them about some issues, teach them about some things in the political arena that they didn't know. But really, their sway, their political identity is already decided. It will come from something their mother taught them years before, a story their grandfather told a million times, where their father worked, etc.

So, here are some things to consider. Where do you work? Do you work at all? What type of role do you play in your household? If you're like me, perhaps your household as an adult, has not always or not yet reached the type of lifestyle your parents raised you in, so your mind is where they raised you, while your day to day is still catching up. Let me explain.

My story is actually a little crazy, but I think I have experienced a variety of things because of it and for that I am grateful. I was born to a single mother who had some hard times. But she was raised in a privileged home, by my grandparents. So, regardless of her social status at present, she spent her whole formative years enjoying a certain way of life. Meanwhile, I spent weekends with those same grandparents and literally knew both lifestyles equally.

Whether through example or literally, my mother raised me to be liberated, independent and maybe a little rebellious. My grandmother taught me to be a homemaker, to find a man, to cook and clean and be accommodating and pleasing. Eventually I would live with my grandmother and for the most part, I have taken the path she put me on, with a few exceptions. I do exude a subservient, traditional female role in my home. But in my single years, I learned independence and inner strength, I acquired an education and had businesses and wrote books. I can switch my mother on and off, but my grandmother always remains. I don't know why.

Did my grandmother's more comfortable lifestyle lead me to believe her way must be better? Was I subconsciously angry with my mother and chose to mimic my grandmother out of spite? So many things we do without knowing the motives or the origin. Something feels right and we lean in that direction.

So, jump to the present. I am a college-educated author. I attend school online and substitute teach as my family time permits. My husband is the head of our household and what he says goes. Now, he is a wonderful man and he makes decisions that are in the best interest of all of us. So kudos to me for my choice, but we do disagree and he does have the final word. At my age, in our society, this is rare. But I'm a Republican. So, are Democrats taking over? Are Republicans a dying breed? Hmmm... not in Kansas.

So what does this have to do with politics? Nothing really. But remember we're trying to see the personal everyday things that show the world and ourselves where we fall on the political tight rope. That small story about my life would lead anyone to believe I am probably a Republican. I won't climb up on a pulpit and crusade about it, because I have laundry to fold and dinner to make. I prefer to be a subdued lady and let my partner lead.

I have a saying... "You know why things were so much better in the 50s? Because things were so much *better* in the 50s!!"

I mentioned the idea that we learn things both intentionally and by example. As much as some may hate to admit it, we absorb things from our parents, good and bad. Some of these things would be ingrained in us, even if we never met a parent. It's a little amazing and a little frustrating. Sometimes we just take for granted that we just are the way we are, when really, if we think about it, every trait we have came from somewhere.

With regard to your personal relationships, your personal life and job, your hobbies, your friends, the way you mold your sons or daughters, or the way you chose not to have sons or daughters, remember two words; Conservative and Liberal.

Synonyms:
(CONSERVATIVE) traditional, old-fashioned, modest, restrained, cautious, reasonable.
(LIBERAL) tolerant, enlightened, radical, progressive, flexible, loose.

I did not dream up these words. They came from a synonym search on the internet. So, when you are describing parts of your life and you're being honest, are you more conservative or liberal?

Once again, this is not meant to lean you in any direction or tell you how to act or not to act. The idea, the point, is that you *already* act how you act. You live how you live. You're either conservative or liberal. Wait, what if you are a mix of both? Are you in the middle? This is a slippery slope, so here's my speech about that. It's ok to be in the middle. We are who we are and that's what makes us and our country so great. I do have some other political parties to introduce to my readers, but with this preface: Know yourself before you introduce all of these possibilities in to your mind. Really think about some of the questions I have asked and know the answers. Don't just claim middle of the road because it's easy.

Please?

When I researched the many political parties in the United States, the list was long, but also full of parties I have never heard of. Obviously Democratic and Republican have been around forever and remain constant. Some parties pop up during certain trends and/or turbulent times and either gain strength or fall away, but still show up on some lists. If you included everyone, the list would be incredibly long and still someone out there would say it was incomplete. So my list is incomplete for sure, but with some descriptions and interesting facts.

Republican… the GOP, the red Elephant, the party on which our country was built, dominating the government from 1860 – 1932. Based on American conservatism and some classical liberalism.

Democratic ... Liberal and progressive, always interested in change, new ways, new solutions. Supporting social liberalism since the 1930s. Today is composed mostly of progressives and centrists. (*What is a Centrist?) It's important to note that the Democratic Party favors modern liberalism, not classic liberalism.

"Class, open your dictionaries..." Centrist: A person whose political opinions are not extreme; a person whose beliefs fall between those of liberals and conservatives. (Merriam-Webster)(Cherilyn says: from the root word center, middle, *fence*.)

Libertarian... started in the 70s during Vietnam. Described by one recent presidential candidate as "more socially liberal than Democrats, but more fiscally conservative than Republicans." The current Libertarian policy positions include; lowering taxes, allowing citizens to opt-out of Social Security, abolish welfare, legalizing drugs and supporting gun rights. Libertarians support homosexual freedom and pornography. (I'm sure the hate mail is on its way, but I don't mince words.)

Green Party... founded in 1984. Emphasizes social and economic justice, grassroots Democracy, non-violence and peace. Sounds great, but there are currently no Green Party members running or holding any state or national offices except one seat in the Arkansas House of Representatives.

Tea (TAXED ENOUGH ALREADY) Party ....a great example of the parties that pop up in different political climates, the Tea Party has been alive for five years and has an article in the New York Times just yesterday (2.27.2014.) The Tea Party has been called extreme Republicans, both agitating and aiding the Republican Party. Three U.S. Senators are from the Tea Party, two of which plan to run for president in 2016.

Please remember, I am not an expert on politics. I am researching as I go, as it is important to me to present the facts and help anyone on their journey for self-exploration and discovery. Luckily, there are many books, websites and television shows out there to help you research further, when you feel yourself leaning towards one party or another. Just doing this research makes me want to read more, know more, understand more. It doesn't mean I will change or my political affiliation will be altered, but I will know more about those around me and that is ALWAYS good!

This book is about the journey of one woman, telling the tale of her own political dance card, how she got there and how others can get there as well. Most especially, that it's very possible and very ok, to believe and be passionate, without spending your life on a soap box. The whole reason I thought to write this book in 2008, is because the looks I would get from people when I told them I was Republican. Anytime I wonder if there are others' out there, struggling with identity of any kind, I feel there is a story to be told.

Relationships

What do your relationships say to the world about your political affiliation? Do you even care? You should and I'll tell you why.

If you're just going on about your life, living and doing and thinking you are not political and it doesn't matter, here's why it does. We have relationships with everyone around us. From our spouses and family to the person that serves our coffee; the principal at our daughter's school and the mail man. Our actions from large to small are absorbed...maybe not scrutinized or examined, but I use the word *absorbed*, very intentionally. It's a passive thing that happens easily and without purpose or agenda. But like the FBI, everyone in our lives have a 'file' for us in their brain and over time, this or that is absorbed into that file and a profile develops. So, who cares right? So they have an opinion about us, big deal.

Ok, but what if that person sees your purse or your phone or hears you talking about your meeting or your knitting. So they decide you are this way or that way and then later they tell someone else or don't vote for your sister on the school board or decide not to go to your housewarming party, not invite your son to Bible Camp, etc. These are all random hypothetical examples, but I am just trying to really bring home the reality, that everything shapes us and our lives, no matter how indifferent we claim to be. We can't help it or stop it, we can just be aware of it. I used the word 'not' a lot, but I wasn't trying to be negative. It can just as easily mean they *do* recommend you for that school board seat, they do 'like' your recipe on Pinterest or they do wave you in line when the traffic is backed up around Target on Saturday.

What *do* my relationships say about me? You've heard about my domestic relationship, but I do have others. I do various things in the community, in a personal, social and professional capacity. There are people I call friends and people I consider to be acquaintances and then some people I literally would not let pump my gas. I'm pretty polite, but I am honest or I figure out a way to avoid a conflict, but I do not bend on those separate groups. I worry about my kids and what they hear, my job(s) and my spouse's job and my position in the community. I worry about grandchildren that aren't born and how my actions today may affect them tomorrow.

I'm not saying we, as people, should tiptoe around and act perfect or anything. I mean if you want to close down the bar on a Tuesday or wear your pajamas to the market or tattoo PEACE on your forehead, you should.

You don't have to care about assumptions or decisions or judgments that may be made, you just have to know they will be made. This applies to wearing your hair in a bun, driving a Volvo and singing in the church choir. The more evolved we all are, the fewer assumptions there will be and the more accurate assumptions will become. I'm sorry... I got distracted by thoughts of utopia again!

Community

It's very unlikely that any one of us can really just contain ourselves within a group of solely like-minded people. I mean unless you are Amish or live in a cult or never leave the house, we have to exist with other people of all walks of life. This is a good thing. It broadens our minds and increases our understanding. We don't have to like or agree or go to coffee, but exposure is always good.

So what does your community say about you and what would your community say about you? Not saying you have to care, but you might be surprised by the answers to those two very different questions. If a friend of mine came from out of town, having never been to my city, he/she would, positively, even if subconsciously, absorb some evaluation about me, based on where I have chosen to live, the people I choose to dwell with, etc. Even people I have never met, live in my vicinity and therefore say something about me. It's just a fact.

So, I say again...

What does your community say about you?
What would people in your community say about you?

The ones that know you?
The ones who have only seen you?
The ones who have heard of you?

If we treat these questions like the ones we asked ourselves about our partners or close family & friends, listening for those key conservative & liberal words, what would we hear?

True story; the other day someone said I was part of the Tea Party. Of course I corrected him (in my most pleasing voice) and said, "No, I'm a Republican."

He said "same thing."

This kills me. I don't care so much that he made an assumption about me, but that the assumption and MANY like it, exist, in excess. But it proves my point. I did nothing to fuel that assumption, but there it is. I knew it was incorrect and I told him and maybe he cares or he doesn't, but I never want to be the person walking around not knowing who I am, not knowing if what people say about me is true or not.

But politics is not something we are always just taught like reading and writing. I mean, you can avoid it in school and at home. You can also seek it out, but you can definitely avoid it. So, through no fault of one's own, we exude one affiliation or another, whether we mean to or not. Awareness is always good. Awareness is the key to everything. Awareness sets you apart.

4

Your Issues & Mine

This is going to be the longest chapter in the book, I can just feel it. There are so many issues we have yet to cover.

Religious Freedom ~ Separation of Church & State

"Hello God? It's me, Republican."

Whether anyone likes it or not, our country was founded on a Christian platform. Everyone was Christian. I mean get up, pray, eat, pray, work all day, pray, go to bed, pray, get up again, pray, always tithe, God fearing Christians. Not just scripture quoting and cross loving, but hard working, sacrificing, simple living people. They knew struggle. They knew hardship and they overcame. God is on our money, in our pledge, in all the documents and in every story of our forefathers. That said, the country has changed and evolved into the melting pot that it is today. There are many religions now and insisting on respect for them all is totally realistic. But is it realistic to try and forget that the reason we have this great country, the reason it has developed into a melting pot, the egg that came before this glorious goose.... was God?

I am a Christian, but a baby one and not a recruiter and again, not trying to convince anyone of anything as far as belief or faith or religion. Those are choices for each person to make individually. But the facts of Christianity's role in our country, our government, our lives, cannot be denied. You don't have to like it.

Ok, I really have point. I would say almost every subject/issue that we cover, can be answered with something biblical. It's true. The problem is, most people that need to hear this, don't want to. The Bible is more than a devotional, it's a history book. This has been proven time and time again. So when I see an issue and I know the solution, I just have to keep my mouth shut, because the minute you bring it up, your issue is lost in it.

As far as religious freedom and the political parties, obviously most of the GOP and some members of the Democratic Party proudly announce their faith, but try to keep it under control when it comes to matters of national importance and policy, simply to abide by the church and state separation regulations. I've never understood removing the church from the state that it created, but no matter. There are many who think very purely about Americans, screaming English and Christianity across the board. These are usually Republicans, but not the educated ones or many in the public eye. But there are probably some very well-known public officials who do feel that way, but would never tarnish their reputation or their chances in office, by saying it out loud. To represent the masses, you have to appeal to them, right or wrong.

But religious freedom really isn't about politicians saying Amen. It's about all people in the United States being able to practice or not practice, whatever religion they choose. Sounds pretty simple right? Enter "Westboro Baptist Church." Not a church at all, but an entity of wise, related attorneys, who have used the laws of religious freedom to do unspeakable things, incite violence and sue for damages. This is just one of the many explanations going around, so I don't attest to the accuracy. But their well-publicized appearances and protests, at the most inappropriate places, acting like anything but Christians, is clear and obvious. That is an example of a law gone wrong, protecting the wrong people, doing exactly the opposite of what was intended.

The separation of church and state began, to prevent all of the people into being forced to practice the same religion. Ok. So we put it in writing and say it's a law. Ok. Really? But everyone is who they are. That includes their faith, their taste, their class and their opinions. Do we really believe they can be unbiased because we type it up? FIVE sitting justices of our current Supreme Court are Catholic. The Dems are pointing this out mercilessly in the recent vote that upheld the rights of Hobby Lobby. So is it true? Can NO ONE put their faith aside and just vote on the facts? If you don't think they can, there's no point in separating church and state. There's no point in separating political parties for that matter.

Westboro is just an example of how 'freedom' can go too far and rights can be taken advantage of. The forefathers called them *unalienable*, but really? In some foreign countries where religion is fairly extreme, everyone follows the same rules, including visitors, including Americans. These include women covering up and acting a certain way in public, men maintaining a hierarchy, etc. In those places, their rules are extreme and yet they are followed. I am not comparing America with war torn places where women and children are mistreated. I'm simply pointing out, their house, their rules.

If we can make a law that says you can only cross on the green, why can't we make more stringent regulations about being included under the broad blanket of religious freedom, instead of handing that privilege to just anybody who throws open a door and sticks a cross in the yard?

The U.S. has lost sight of the word privilege and instead calls everything a *right*. I have the right to live and die. That's about it. (And that first one is iffie.)

Gay Rights/Marriage

In 2008, when I wrote my outline for this book, this heading only said Gay Marriage. It's six years later and this is still an issue, but really the topic has widened and so I included Gay Rights. I'm sure there are lots of other subtitles we can include in there, but I promise to be thorough.

There are countless reasons why the gay community has run into opposition in our society. They are 'different' and therefore resisted. Could it really be that simple? By simple, I mean naïve? Primitive? I am a quiet Republican and a Christian, but I still want to be intelligent and logical in my opinions. There are religious reasons, ideas about what is normal and what is not, etc. There are various definitions of marriage and family. Then there's an entirely separate, but just as loud spectrum on the financial side of it. Many people's opinions on gay rights are 100% fiscally motivated, meaning they don't want to have to pay for more family insurance, life insurance, medical leave, spousal benefits, etc. To think that those people are not out there is just blind ignorance.

All that said, I am a Republican and a Christian. I believe the bible, but the part of the bible I hear the loudest, is "thou shalt not judge." The only truly accurate interpretation of the bible is by God himself and until we meet him we are just making educated guesses. So in the absence of absolute proof, shouldn't we not judge? Maybe all the gay people that are getting married are sinning. Maybe they'll all go to hell. Maybe they're evil and maybe they'll be punished. I have no idea. Not my problem, so I don't care if they get married.

There are those who insist that it is their business because it is affecting our society, our world, etc. But everything does. I also don't agree with nose piercing, ear gauging, some people's parenting, foul language, houses painted purple and sofas on front porches. But this is America. So I can be tolerant and realistic that there are millions of people with millions of opinions or I can stay home, pull down the shades and order in. I have homosexual friends. I have friends who drink too much. I have friends who have had abortions. I have friends who make tons of poor decisions. We are all flawed. I don't judge. It doesn't mean I am ok with any of it.

Once again I address rights vs. privileges. I do not think companies should have to provide anything but fair wages and conditions. Perks are perks. Some benefits are better than others. Plenty of jobs offer none. That's life. Get a better job. Pay cash.

Death Penalty

Rights & Privileges. Life is a privilege. Free, wealthy society is a privilege. Clean water, good food, safe neighborhoods and free police protection...all privileges. Like I mentioned before...we all get police, courts, etc. Even people who don't pay taxes, who aren't citizens. So are they rights or privileges?? If you can't play nice and follow the rules, then you can't hang out in our playground. Wow this chick is crazy right?

She didn't mention life!
She didn't mention God?
She didn't use the word murder.

Of course life is very important, the most important. But life is full of injustices. I could get hit by a bus or struck by lightning tomorrow. That would be unfair, but I would be dead nonetheless. People walking around killing, torturing and otherwise victimizing one another is on them! They made their bed so let them sit in a chair.

Affirmative Action

Is this even a real thing anymore? I think companies should hire who they want, for the reasons they want. Someone built that company from the ground up. That's their blood, sweat and tears and they should decide who wears their name and represents them to the world. Period. Guess what, I run two very small companies and I have one child who requires employees that I hire and fire. That's my child they're taking care of, my baby. And my companies, they feed my children, they keep our lights on. So if someone's appearance or voice or outfit or attitude or ANYTHING turns me off. No job for you. It's not personal, to them. It's very personal to me.

Men & Women...in the workplace, in the home, in the military, etc. remember .... only YOU really have to live with you...we're not talking about laws or modern policies, opinions, etc.... only you know the real ideas living in between your ears...but really, they live in your heart and they can be hard to hide. So who wants a job they had to ride in on their platform, their soapbox or their local policy? You don't think your co-workers resent you? You think anyone will ever respect you? How about being hired on merits?

I know, I know.... But I said employers should be able to hire whomever they want, right? So what about their idiot nephew or the secretary they're sleeping with? People. Life is rough. Those things will ALWAYS exist, but guess what? If YOU are hired because of your gender or your race, you are no different than the secretary and the nephew. So who do you want to be?

Immigration

I am feeling, sounding redundant, I know. But if I leave something out, then I get yelled at.

    Warning: Cherilyn   does   not   like
yelling. (qR)

I totally get that America is a melting pot, but we weren't always. When the Native Americans inhabited parts of North America, it was not the United States and it was not any other established society either. It was a lot of land. We made it the place that it became in 1776. It was far from a melting pot in 1776. Lots of places are melting pots, but few start out that way. We are being punished for our generosity. Some people are confusing privileges, gifts, their lucky fifty stars!!!...with rights....again.

Let's say Jane was born poor. She lives in a shack and just across the tracks little Johnnie was born rich. This is chance or luck on their part....probably very intentional acts and good or bad choices on their parents' parts, but their lot in life regardless. So should Jane just be able and stomp her foot and insist on moving into the mansion? Of course not. That would seem ridiculous to anyone. So why should someone in one country, ANY country or neighborhood or house, just be able to whine and get a better life? Guess what? There is torture and rape and injustice and poverty in America. We do our best to police and protect. There are rich people in Mexico and India and Iran and China. So, opportunities and dangers exist everywhere. You either rise to the top or you don't. That's life.

It blows my mind that the local gymnasium has a limit on occupants, due to safety, space, etc. But the United States cannot have such a limit. Dumb.

5

Searching for George
(Washington that is.)

Once again when I think about the forefathers, the Constitution, the Bill of Rights, I am reminded of the Bible. These are all documents written hundreds or more years ago, by individuals who may have been speaking a similar language, but may not have been in the same context, frame of mind or made up at all like you and me. But still, billions of people spend every day following the rules and ways outlined within them. The fact is, words on a piece of paper will never, ever give us the answers we really need to know. We are constantly searching, interpreting and enforcing what we hope George Washington and his peers had in mind. Are we anywhere close? Interpretation is relative and we are each one of us so incredibly different. The mere idea that we could be totally off, is terrifying.

But the people that run our country are smart, adult, well-read and the list goes on. Surely even left to their own devices they must be doing ok. Right?

We. Will. Never. Know.

Be careful what you wish for.

Why?

Because the truth is, we don't know what was going on in the minds of our forefathers. We have only the written word. I hold much reverence for the written word, but back then, even their English was different than ours. What did they mean by unalienable rights? Bread and water or DVRs and cellular phones? We already know that every man being equal was a relative term, so what else have we misunderstood?

George Washington was an anti-interventionist. He believed we should keep to ourselves and let other governments worry about themselves. Amen.

My point is this. We do a lot of things in the name of our Constitution, our forefathers, the American Dream, etc... but all of those terms and those people left instructions that if we are honest, we cannot possibly interpret. So before we wish for things or dreams or a way of life that we have heard about, we may stop and remember that we really don't know what we're talking about. Or rather, we know what we're talking about, but we will really never know what they were.

Republican Women & Republican Men

"Is she suggesting that Republicans should be described as separate beings, based on their sex? But there are no differences between men and women, of any political affiliation!"

Right?

Oh but there are, like everything else involving the sexes, there is always a difference. Of course with Republican men & women, their differences fold together like parallel lines and they are exactly as they should be. I am not suggesting only in relationships or marriages, although they certainly manifest there as well, but in office, at work, in school and in society, Republican men & women function well, together and apart. Ironically, the peace loving Democrats pale in comparison.

Democrats try to wear all the hats. This is just silly and unrealistic. There are many roles in the world and there are those who are suited for them. There is nothing wrong with that, but Democrats shake their fists at anything defining anyone person or group. They are so dead set against labels that they refuse to accept that accurate labels are helpful, productive and natural.

Of course there are exceptions to every rule, but we must accept and embrace that the rule exists! There are women in the military, law enforcement and kick boxing, but there is a logical and obvious reason why they are not there in high numbers. This goes the same for men in grade school teaching, nursing and housekeeping. Neither of these lists are more important than the other. They simply are. The differences, good and bad, between men and women, have nothing to do with equality, but more with reality. Like an apple and an orange, both important and wonderful, but nevertheless, different. Orange pie would not be good and apples will not cure a cold. No one need protest.

Republican men and women, even in office and positions of power, have long followed an example of tradition and conservatism. This is why they are the *Grand Old Party*. They have persevered and survived. They must be doing something right.

So, if we have accurately or even just intelligently decided what George and his buddies had in mind, where does that leave us? Why are we not trying to preserve those ideals? Why are the people trying to build on what was the best plan for a society, trying to get back to that, being persecuted? The more we move away from those original ideals, the more problems we have. This is not a coincidence. I mean really folks, who can dispute that? The more we rebel against the good things that our forefathers started, the deeper in turmoil our country has become. Is everyone blind to that connection?

I'm not saying we should have slavery, that women shouldn't vote or that teachers should wack everybody with sticks. There's a difference between allowing natural progress and allowing deterioration. I change my house as the years pass. I update my appliances, I choose new colors as trends travel through, but my foundation, my walls, the dynamics that build a house, have never changed. I do not scream "freedom" and then go drill holes in the floors and fill the walls with water, just because I can. Just because we have the freedom to do things doesn't mean we should and doesn't mean there still aren't some really ignorant ideas out there.

6

Times They Are A Changin...

Surviving Republican

As the world progresses, progressively, where are we? Of course when I say we, I mean myself and fellow Republicans, but in truth, everyone has to ask themselves this question. Will your group survive? Forget the political parties, their names and their mascots. Will your group of like-minded people, whatever their beliefs, keep hold of their little niche in our society? Does it matter?

Does it?

Some would say, of course it matters. Everything we do, big or small, creates a chain reaction that potentially affects everyone and the world right? Well, maybe, but really. If I vote, I vote. Ideally, all of my fellow thinkers vote similarly and that makes our unity important. But would we still all vote that way if we had never met, commiserated and shook our fists at our collective political enemies? Isn't that in itself a problem? When people join in fellowship, for any common cause or interest, isn't it human nature that their opinions and ideas will be swayed? Perhaps they are educated, enlightened in parts of the issue that they were previously unaware? So this would be a good course of change. But what if their cohorts are incorrect, blatantly lying, influenced by emotion and peddling jargon they too swallowed blindly? Perhaps the masses are not the forum in which to make decisions.

At the end of the day, survival is really not a concern.

"What? What is she talking about? We MUST survive!!"

No. No, not really. *I* will survive, *you* will survive, but *we* really don't need to survive. Our definition of *we* changes from day to day. It's that draw to be in a group, the safety in numbers, the peer pressure, that form these groups to begin with. They are NOT necessary. I promise. qR

The fact is, no two Republicans, or Democrats, Libertarians or flamingoes are alike. Try as they may to be united, we are all human and unique. Have your views changed since you have taken up with a group of political comrades? I bet they have. And why is that? Have their views changed since being around you? It's impossible for that answer to be no. Whether these changes are dramatic and political or subtle and more about human nature, we all respond to our surroundings. Has this book changed one tiny, regimented idea you used to hold dear?

Are politics really politics, or is it just another reason for people to get together?

The world is changing. The United States is changing. More and more, the greatest movements are invariably for change, diversity and modern thinking. Can there be a modern, Republican point of view. Can there be a way to preserve the seventeenth century and still thrive in the twenty-second? Yes. (what did you expect me to say?)

I love metaphors and I love getting back to basics. There's only one way to bake a cake. I mean seriously. Flour, eggs and water, right? Of course a few things can vary, add some pecans, subtract some egg yolk, but from the Quakers to Martha Stewart, cake is cake. Ovens evolve, metal pans turn into silicone, cakes can even look like cars and dinosaurs and virtually anything you desire. But they are still cake. Having grown and progressed with the times, it is still relevant and recognized, but cake is still cake.

Let's be cake! We have to embrace modern realities, but we just have to be creative and steadfast and find a way to do that, without changing our conservative ideals.

What about the next generation? Do we raise our children Republican, as if there is no other option; or do we lay our cards on the table and give them choices? Do you view your political stance as serious as your religion or as flexible as your favorite flavor of ice cream? There is the answer. If you believe being a Republican or a Democrat, or a Christian or an electrician makes you a better person, a better member of society, a better mother... you will kill yourself trying to instill the same in your child.

On the other hand, if these choices came to you on a breeze and you think other affiliations may be just as happy, correct and moral, you may just throw Junior out of the nest and see where he lands.

For Republicans specifically, this decision is MORE important. WE are old school. We are preserving history, George Washington, centuries of governmental and social evolution. We cannot be complacent and take the chance of that dying with us or our children. This is why *most* Republicans, are not quiet.

Other titles by Cherilyn G. Hearn...

Two Sides Of Wilde
The Senator's Daughters
Faces Of The Poor Farm
My Daughter Still
Creepy Christina
Aunt Snow

Coming Soon....

Far From The Tree
Safe In The Middle
By Alice Owen

.